By the Nest

Kathi Morrison-Taylor

Kathi Morrison-Taylor

Dear Ellen,
Thank you for your
friendship and
support. I hope
you continue to
explore your
own poetic
voice.
love,
K.
11/8/08

THE WORD WORKS
HILARY THAM CAPITAL COLLECTION
WASHINGTON, D.C.

First Edition   First Printing
By the Nest
Copyright © 2009 by Kathi Morrison-Taylor

The WORD WORKS
PO Box 42164
Washington, DC 20015
editor@wordworksdc.com

Cover art: "Yard" by Grier Torrence

Book design, typography by Janice Olson
Printed by Signature Book Printing, www.sbpbooks.com

Library of Congress Control Number: 2008928432
International Standard Book Number: 0-915380-69-2
ISBN 13: 9780915380695

ACKNOWLEDGMENTS

Grateful acknowledgment is due the editors of the following publications in which versions of these poems have appeared:

Calyx: "On Heritage Night at My Children's Elementary School"

Emrys Journal: "A Beauty"

Harpur Palate: "Diagram of the Female Reproductive System, Translated"

Innisfree Poetry Journal: "Back Walkover," "Tomatoes," "Bad Dog, Memory," "Pile of Discarded Shoes"

Mirror Northwest: "Tooth Fairy," "Continuing Education," "Eat and Learn," "Moose Heart"

The Pedestal: "Seth"

Potomac Review: "Hula Hoop"

River City: "Disappearance"

Southern Poetry Review: "Angels and the Real Thing"

Stand: "First Steps"

"Hermit Crab" and "Cucumber" appeared on posters throughout the Northern Virginia Metro system as part of the 2005 and 2008 Moving Words program.

I would like to express my appreciation to the teachers, friends, and colleagues who have encouraged me over the last 20 years, from graduate degree to first book. By the Nest *is especially indebted to Marie Ponsot and the XY Group who nurtured ideas at the core of these poems and to Molly Peacock whose wisdom and kindness compelled me to take a deep breath, dust myself off, and carry on.*

My heartfelt thanks also goes to Karren Alenier, Sandra Beasley, and the team of generous editors at The Word Works for believing in my work, and to Grier Torrence for allowing me to use his artwork on the cover.

CONTENTS

I...

II...

III...

IV...

V...

For my family

I

Ultrasound—the Sole of His Foot

The camera invades his privacy.
My son squirms away, shifts in his elastic sea,
pushes off the tissue and muscle
that constrains and consoles from the beginning.

His foot presses up against the wall of me,
as though I were below, looking up
through a crinkled, cellophane ceiling,
where his black and white heart beats

and his tiny toes press ten steady marks
on the screen. Technicians measure
his body, as superstitiously I foresee
his inclination to retreat.

Once in a heated argument, my mother said
she never really knew me. Her eyes red and teary
ensured she couldn't see herself in my face,
but I still feel the pinch of her looking.

First Steps

from Picasso's painting First Steps

This morning when her body bends
over her toddler she is a half-
curled embryo releasing a birth
in blue. How is it after
almost a year he continues to move
out of her? Her own birth is impossible
to remember, cubes dark as mystery.
For now she trusts him. Though
she expects the words "Let go"
at this separation—left foot raised,
balance sure—the words don't come
yet, only short cries she interprets
as delight. She is a Madonna
of linear discipline. Her hands cup
her child's as his foot falls
forward to test a new audience.
His chin is a full circle
she kisses after.

Bubbles

Not quite invisible,
a curve defines their birth.
They take your trace of breath, to burst

somewhere without word or flesh
or crash. A vessel gone,
your puff released. No longer caged

in sphere, but atmosphere. Droplets
fall away, as the next lung-tickling
membrane's cusp completes itself,

out and up,
an escape as clean
as light is clear.

A Beauty

Late harvest; nothing sour remains
in this strawberry field. I pick,

wary of rot and small bites rabbits make
when evening settles on U-Pick acres

and forest spreads its shadows thick as jam.
But now the sun is high and nibblers shy away

from women and children who come to kneel
in this grid of vines. Beside me,

a little boy learns which to pick.
His mother nods at a good choice, says,

"That's a beauty." He repeats, "A beauty."

"Beauty," all down the row, the warm
pulse-curved fruit in his fist.

He sings, "A beauty," as if calling for a pet
before he stoops to look again.

Wind teases leaves back, a gentle
echo to his wish. Is it summoning his future?

A beauty that is his black eye
three years from now? A beauty hit

to soar past outfielders? A beauty
who sits behind him in high school

chemistry? Scarlet flashes beneath the green.
I lift the vine to take an answering shape:

a double berry, firm-hipped and promising.
Farther up the row, again he finds

the crayon-red sweet thing
he has learned to search for.

Sea Monkeys

My daughter rips the foil packet
and pours tenants into the tank—
as directions say, INSTANT PETS.
Eggs like pearly dandruff hatch
into jiggling specks. On the package
a cartoon brine shrimp winks.

They grow, endear themselves
to my child. Daily, she aerates the tank—
pours greenish water from glass to glass—
provides powdered algae clumped
smaller than mustard seed.
Little water chimps agitate
for breakfast at the surface,

so human in their neediness and spunk,
they earn the playful name we offer:
Sea Monkeys. What if, magnified,
we too might invite analogy?
Something generous, far cuter
than our small, mean selves?

Recognition at Candlemas

Luke 2: 34–35

Rings of white paper skirt white candles,
catching tears of wax. We pass the flame

as the chaplain reads about Anna
and Simeon who recognized Jesus

the way I at once recognized my own firstborn,
someone imagined so deeply

I could not conceive her as new,
rather someone so long expected

I already knew her. In the temple
in the heart of Jerusalem,

did Mary sigh, over-full of predictions?
What made her so patient with the old prophets?

Unlikely nurses, they purified her,
that duo of seers sagging with wisdom.

In their comfort, they predicted her pain,
a sword through her soul, yet the thoughts of many hearts

to be revealed. Babies hiccup, burp,
and yawn into their histories. Grandparents

bow over an infant, perfect as a doll
once held in childhood as a hearth died down

to ash—ash imagined just warm to the touch.
Candle wax soft on the paper in my hand.

Eat and Learn

Four vinyl placemats on our kitchen table,
bear the motto *Eat and Learn*—multiplication facts,
a world map, the Jurassic Age, and a view
of all nine planets orbiting—
because we on Earth are messy.

Boy quizzes girl, "Spell *Kazakhstan.*"
A milk glass rests on eight-times-eight.
The table shakes as if answers wiggle
under breakfast plates. Food for thought:

Old friends flung far to the world—
Congo and Cambridge—joined by a dribble of sauce;
the island of Singapore a sticky dot
where a playmate moved last summer.

Cranky grown-ups scoot in chairs, slice fruit,
watch as colored spots and opaque ocean
suffer knife-fork-napkin archeology.
A little fist wraps a Clementine moon,

peeled to divide; scrim of grape jelly,
eye of an egg over easy, just barely closed.
Calories keep us from falling apart, wake us
to these moments of trivia and life,
our brains, groggy stars, hungry and rising.

My Daughter in the Garden

What is real, she meets on all fours—
ants circle hollyhocks,
nails spike one edge of the gazebo.

Her fingers weave like baby snakes
through the woodpile; dirt powders her nose.
No notion of caution, she tastes the rocks,

salty as blood, the flavor of shadow,
half-past two. Now she mouths
the sundial's chipped pedestal,

until fingers scribble
under her ribs, pull her up
from all fours back to breast.

Before Alejandra Pulls Her Turnips

Here baby's breath fills the rows
between vegetables. The white flowers shine
a frill of light, become a hub for bees.

Million Stars and Bristol Fairy bloom in the kindergarten plot,
tiny white flowers among Joy's dill and Tom's beans;
delicate and skeletal, it separates.

Sprigs of infant air, scientific name *Gypsophila*.
Write it with marker on a popsicle stick for the child
who can read. She thinks of gypsies, whirling,

shaking tambourines above her turnips still too small to pull,
gold coins and cloudy crystals offering heart's desire.
No botanist or ancient scholar handy to tell her

Gypso comes from *gypsum*, whiter than white,
the color of the light outside the womb,
when a seed breaks through earth into the sun's

domain and *phila* is love, the way dirt embraces roots
all snuggled down in the new turned bed.
Imagine her old-world vegetable drinking in some purple,

aging into its colorful self, a bulb unaware
of space just above where harvesters dance.
Dance, dance among lacy breathing.

Seth

Last born, he is just a whisper
in Genesis. Between passages
Eve's form grows lighter,
her bones free to bear only herself.

Kneeling, she pins love reserves to his sleeve,
sends him daily into a field of voices,
stories of the weightless life that filled
his parents. Imprints of God's lips,

a breeze Eve can hardly recall,
ripple the grain until even crows
seem to pine. Scythes rise on their own
to meet their task, the rye.

One day some creatures Adam never named
find Seth alone by water.
They admire how stones fall so easily
from his hands. They lick at his ripples,

and nibble moss roses on the riverbank.
Crawling up his shoulder,
they buzz in his ears. Seth rests,
rehearsing soft sounds they made.

He imagines his brothers
alive again. He hums
the verse to a close. The world
grows large with children.

II

Tooth Fairy

Speechless and secretive as God,
she accepts their doubt. I wouldn't know
what to do without her (gory gaps
somehow lessened by a handful of change)—
how to explain that first discovered
loss of self, how to reassure
eyes won't fall out next or ears wither.

My children treasure the quarters she leaves.
I wish for her as my hair turns gray.
With magic she buys back bits of body,
intervenes as humans age,
makes light of bloodshed.
It's up to me to act on her behalf,
spirit away incisors and bicuspids.

I hoard the evidence, enslaved
by motherhood. I cannot bear to throw away
their tiny nubs, milk-white and faintly stained.
Teeth gather in my jewelry box,
a witchdoctor's jackpot, where ticket stubs,
charms, and chains tangle around them
on their velvet bed, red as a womb.

Back Walkover

I think of prayer. The slow reach up
and curl back, leg rising steadily,
a knobby arm of a clock; then time
tumbles—like that. Seven-year-olds looping
across blue-carpeted sprung floor.

The reason to stretch so far seems complex,
gesture surprising and off-hand.
Each spine answers the will
of an arc, pearls concealed so the arch
is more like a tree bent back by ice

or wind, not the necklace of bone
hung from skull to seat, contorted
into architecture. It's natural.
Their bodies bend before age trains
them back from the ledge where flips and dives

command at least a try. I can still
imagine perfect faith, the breath that fills
my lungs as I look up and back
into the center of God, or just loyal sky
wheeling to catch our dizzy *amens*.

Red Sled

I have my doubts.
At the top of the ice-slick slope,
my five-year-old begs
for his first solo ride.
He tells me where I ought to point his sled
to miss the tree and hit the jump.

Another parent, down below,
waves encouragement
with purple gloves.
The sheet of ice is a sheer page
that the red sled will barely scratch—
no trace of the lung-rush

or galloping speed that words can't stop.
He settles on the sled, a shallow boat,
steered by weight. I hold the yellow
nylon rope. He grips his toy, cries out, *Go,*
and I send him down the ridge.
I've done it.

The yells are mine, as crooked skids
and unintended dips align him with a ditch
of jagged rocks. I've done it.
Before the trench, they separate,
sled and body, so one speeds onward
bouncing gaily, free of purpose,

while the other skids to a stop.
We are that journey apart.
Tumbling down the hill, I find him
safe and crying for his sled,
run farther than young eyes can reach
across the snowy scene, something

a parent must see and retrieve,
a drop of blood beneath a pine tree.

Egret Tree

Perched on white pine
they are white presents,
festive offerings off-season,
fruit feathered and hatched,
hearts born where pits might be.
With tucked faces they sleep
ten on one tree,
abundant wonder.

On Heritage Night at My Children's Elementary School

I show up with brownies, nothing exotic or ethnic
or spicy, no soul food, fried rice, or plantains.
In a Betty Crocker pyramid, I display my dark, sugary fix
awkwardly, pretending a wholesome, American heritage,

while inside, I am the dilute white of my father's alcoholic amnesia,
a translucent fog as homogenous as a mild cold.
I show up with brownies out of a box, whisked with oil,
eggs and water, the color of brandy in his morning coffee,

dense and slightly under-baked. I set them on a table in the gym
wondering what others will think of me, wondering
what I think of them. In an addict's kingdom that's how you think,
sizing up others, who like you, may hear *heritage* and know

Jack Daniels, gin, or a six-pack could as easily appear as this array
of international casseroles. In a United Nations' stew of young
        families,
screw my historic English, Swedish, Scottish, French blood lines.
Our parents teach us what to do, or not to do, in my case.

Marco Polo Arrives Poolside

Arlington, Virginia

Children toss his name out again and again
in an unwitting séance of sun and splash:
Marco—Polo, Marco—Polo.
His spirit's called to summer here.

On the edge of the second millennium,
gazing down into magic-blue chlorine,
in the wealthiest nation, a lifeguard sees how
one child, eyes shut, wades waist-high, yells

Marco, groping at the air playfully, while four others
dodge and dive and tease, nearly naked,
Polo—Polo—Polo—Polo
answering, almost spirit voices—bells like silk

and irreverent laughter. Exploration reduced
to a game of tag. Crossing the Gobi to reach Cathay,
these same careless demons led travelers astray.
Words flung in from a sea of sand—deadly blind man's bluff.

I hand Marco a pool-sized martini, and invite him to stay:
great-tiled walls, a green plastic sword, a globe of onion.

On Listening to My Daughter Practice Schumann's Happy Farmer on Her One-Eighth-Sized Violin

Schumann himself suffered depression
without Lithium or Prozac or Zoloft.
Perhaps that's why he inebriated
his Landsmann in a sunny key;
imagined his whistling merrily,
bouncing across the music staff,
treble steps below the silo,
through a shining black and white harvest
into new chocolate-brown
fields rich with melody.

Beginners play this.
My little girl, not unmusical,
cries while difficult measures
fall away more slowly than she'd like.
Bow drawn to bridge, her violin
whimpers—young animal fumbling
below the straightest line of turnips,
feast just out of reach.
So much practice required
to make the heart light.

Bach's 21st

Some say Bach fathered twenty, not recognizing me.
Much bloodier than opera and healthy,
I entered.   No one recorded my birth date,
my private cry muted, a dim minor key.
In the falsetto of little children,
it's easy to lose count.   Many of us died in infancy.

I never knew brothers and sisters
as well as I knew fugues and canons.
Music wrapped around my days—
the minuets that danced me into teens,
gigues that traveled far yet always stayed with me.
They echoed in strangers' memories but wiggled
my fingers and toes, affectionate
and lively. Melody shuns the grave.

It springs like seasons into wedding's eve or
baptismal shade.   If Father wrote some as elegies,
he never taught me his unwelcome grief.
Chords flew up the organ's throat
and into courts of bows and curtsies, and I
watched the pipes and hummed in sympathy.
The last body from his body, I
knew *quiet* would never be certain,

only a space where notes could quiver, I knew
his studious trance, the music staff
ephemeral, despite nobility's purse,
and I knew Mother knew those visceral notes.
Sometimes I heard her sing as long ago,
under her breath, a twilight squeezing me,
our submerged artistry swimming,
gold-finned aria, quickening to *Allegretto*.

Hula Hoop

A kindergarten Saturn,
she orbits the yard,
fighting physics,
arms raised skyward,
chin tipped up,
eyes shut like a gospel
singer whose lyrics rest
on the tip of grace.

I guess it's about bones
and balance. The body
hoops with soul and smoothes
its hips and ribcage
into a limber pole.
The planets hula
around a muscular sun.

Pink, orange, and green stripes
spiral around my daughter.
She's in outer space,
too busy to recall
how she learned to keep
her circle circling
around one steady
center all her own.

Diagram of the Female Reproductive System, Translated

Both parents born in El Salvador, the neighbor boy, Enrique,
has trouble with his homework, knocks on our door, asking for
my husband's bilingual expertise. At twelve, he must study the
reproductive system in a special class called Health. He hands
my husband a cross-section of a woman, a map with arrows
and blanks. Shyly, he says his parents know only the Spanish
words—tranquil in their living room, listening to the news under
a wide-eyed portrait of Jesus, while their boy in the next apart-
ment learns to pronounce *clitoris, vagina*, and *uterine lining*.
What would Jesus do, faced with a worksheet like this? I find
I need to leave the room so men can talk as men. My husband
comes to consult me only when he is unsure about *fallopian tubes*.
In a half an hour, they are almost done. Anatomically correct and
American, the diagram has filled with terms doctors use. I can
hear Enrique thanking my husband: *Gracias, gracias, gracias,
señor.* His gratitude seems too great, as if he could know that
when you learn a new word in no time you find it everywhere.

Tea Rose Collection

Orange Elf, Love Knot, Plum Frost, Nice Day,
Magic Dragon, Lady Bird, Botticelli, Good-as-gold,
Key Largo, Frankly Scarlet, Othello, Firefall,
Blush Hip, Daddy's Pink, Evangeline, Satchmo,
Henry Ford, Hi Ho, Sangria, Waxwing,
Paddiwack, Faint Heart, Rabble Rouser, Vanity.

Tomatoes

My sloppy work makes me cringe.
I planned to stake them but they grew
too quickly. Now with florists' wire
and strong bamboo, I devise a plan
to raise their fruit, pull the dragging
arms erect without splintering limbs.
Most say they're delicate,
and it's true that at twilight you can't
water them without risking blight,

but don't discount their unruly ways:
Beefsteak tomatoes strain stems
until they rest in bush beans, cherry tomatoes
tempt moles with dusty spice,
and Big Boys in our corner plot tease
sharp eyes, flash orange beacons
under watermelon vine. They wax wild
like the teenage girls I teach.
Next year, I will cage them quick,

before they know July sun,
encircle each seedling with wire hoops,
fair boundaries for enthusiasm.
They will grow upright, aligned in rows,
tendrils trained efficiently. They'll perform
as I ask them to—unlike my girls,
who tend themselves appallingly,
prop their breasts with Wonder bras,
and bare their midriffs to the summer's heat.

Cucumber

Only the skin is ugly,
an armor against slugs and rot.
Inside is the newest pastel,
a color like noon sky where
it brushes the sun's glare, the last
moist swipe of cool before the burn.
On your eyelids, thin slices
wither, and seeds glisten
their melancholy balm.

Vinegar

Victorian ladies drank it,
a tonic to keep their complexions
white. I imagine,
they gulped it quick-like.

All-purpose stain-lifter, it saves me.
Our bath tile's mildew free—
grout cleansed back to ivory.
I've killed my appetite.

The very cruet enchants me,
diamond-fine, pure as a faint.
But the scent stings, salt in a scrape,
bad medicine, sharper

than corset bones beached and weathered
on imperial sand.

Hermit Crab

She makes each shell her own,
despite its shape or color.
She lives alone as any living thing
within its skin. Thinking thoughts
of water or of land, she shifts the sand
with each step toward the ocean.

Naturalization

The Laotian mechanic sits on our couch and tells me about my fifteen-year-old cat, how she has a reason to have stayed with us for so long, how he can see it in her whiskered face. He has just finished working on our brakes, and we'll now help him proof his immigration papers, but the cat talks to him. I can see that. She is a noisy, tortoise-shell cat. He pets her and tells about a family back in his homeland, the father's tragic death, but, wait, before that the father, sensing misfortune, buried the family's riches in a secret place. A stray dog came to live with the impoverished widow, shortly after her husband's passing. She knew to take care of the dog, to give it the best meat and softest bedding. Sure enough, in two months, the dog led the family to its money. Our mechanic scratches the cat's head; he is a sad Buddhist. I know some of his story: how he came to America twenty years ago with his wife, a cook for the embassy, their small children. Now his wife won't speak to him, his boys are in the U.S. Army, his youngest girl disappeared after high school and left him with a granddaughter. Long ago he should have dealt with the INS, naturalized before he gathered too many addresses, too many job histories. He tells me to revere my cat, an old soul with good reasons for staying.

Volunteer

I.

A volunteer begonia has rooted itself
between our patio bricks this fall,
a pinky finger of misplaced promise.

Clearing away cast-off leaves, I find
its single, heroic bloom, like a silk boutonniere
from June's last wedding, a nuptial splash

in the cayenne, squash, turmeric mix
of Indian summer. I grasp its quick surprise,
wish away the darkening days.

II.

In a news photo after the Gulf hurricane,
two men walk north on a bleak interstate
carrying a sousaphone. (I think of all the times

I'd wondered what I'd take in fire,
storm or quake.) The horn twists
into a washed grey sky, a nautilus

out of the flood, tarnished, a grand machine.
Its brass holds the shoulders that shudder
to weep, a fossil symphony.

Restoration Piece

The neighbor's snagged a bargain—
a wicker chair for her front stoop.
Once light green, its seat, back, and arms
peel too easily, leave a trail
from car to porch, where I spy her
with a scrub brush massaging
the chair as though it were a horse.

Her own body raw with poison ivy,
neck and forearms flaking,
she knows natural setbacks,
but still flicks her wrist
with each brisk stroke, as slowly
dun fiber surfaces and smoothes
its way free of ornament.

Then she waves to me,
where I stand staring, a clear view
across our boundaries—porch to porch.
She exclaims on the trendy look
(that paint-flecked rash of imperfection)
affection broadcast in her voice,
the commandment: renew.

IV

My Children Dyeing Easter Eggs

Armed with sponge and detergent,
I watch them stain their fingertips
with the fizzy vinegar color-kit—
blue, yellow, pink, and green dye.
They bob eggs on a copper hoop,

some super-sized IUD—
a spring ritual to contemplate
living and dying, their arts and crafts.
Carefree drips over want ads and funnies.
Color is the rush that heaves the boulder free,
the hen's egg my son turns robin's-egg blue,
to match a sky, stunning and empty.

Disappearance

Standing between fields of red tulips,
I miss my father. It is Easter,
and bees ascend into a sun
glaring to dim shapes.

New form seems possible
in their soft, humming
flight, new purpose with wings
drawn up and out

from scarlet flowers.
My eye follows crimson
waves to vanishing
point, where sky meets

field, light clouds feather,
then this armload
of cut flowers is lifted close,
closer to disappearance.

Continuing Education

At my father's funeral, an elderly woman,
close-cropped gray hair and sparkling eyes,
took me by the arm. She had been a member
of his figure drawing class, the one that heard
about the car crash

as they'd gathered the morning-after for their session.
She asked me if my father spent his childhood years
in Pasco, and when I answered yes, she said that
she had always suspected but never said anything.
She had been

his fourth-grade teacher back then, when he had been
just as creative and intelligent, she said. It would have
made my father laugh—the eighty-year-old sketching
nudes in his class, holding back her identity.
His laughter cannot belong to me.

Angels and the Real Thing

You wait for the bus
in your best purple dress.
The sky begins
to tumble to night.

The police cannot stop it
with hot silver whistles.
The judge pounding his gavel
only shatters the clouds.

Above you two women
wash windows,
water geraniums,
thin pitcher spouts

sprouting water onto flowers,
long transparent fingers
wetting red and white petals,
turning soil black.

Dripping from the window box,
a rain that smells of roots.
One woman says:
"The baby is sick again."

The other answers:
"My prayers to Elizabeth; bless
her patience." And the bus
is coming. Rolling the pavement,

rumbling to a stop, it's ready for you.
In an old movie this could mean
you're dying. The driver smiles down,
his name could be Peter.

And those women up there,
they could be angels.

Playing Our Birthdays

Not because he loved her, but because of habit,
Mom would say. When years after the divorce
he played her birthday, mine, and his for the jackpot.
He held on to what he felt was luck
long after she packed her bags and left him.
Even their anniversary splashed its date
onto losing tickets that he never threw away,
dozens discovered in old sports coats' pockets.
As if their man-and-wife collision
could mean nothing less than a ridiculous fortune,
our union as a family fixed in numerology—
three-in-one destined for fame.
As if some rational good should finally come
of the days, months, and years that dropped us here
together, and left us, once knotted in dismay,
slowly working apart.

Moose Heart, 1973

Larger than a human heart and frozen
it stood in a roasting pan at the center of our circle.
As our third-grade teacher, Mr. Carbone,
dissected the moose heart, he probed with a knife tip
into vocabulary—*left ventricle, right atrium,*
aorta, arteries, veins.

He asked us to consider how it looked like our hearts.
And I did. We all listened to him,
a peacenik in a mustard-yellow cardigan.
Watching the purple gore melt,
I felt my insides sink closer to the floor.
Cold space filled my stomach

until my ears began to buzz.
I fought a faint. I didn't want to imagine
the core of my body, bloody
and barred by ribs, four chambers, flesh valves,
capillaries that webbed into extremities,
regressed into invisibility on a steel blade.

I knew my heart was safe, but this one,
opened and dead, sent me sadness
that thrummed through my limbs,
sent me sadness that knew my blood and said
agony, agony. Who could ignore
each frayed nerve absorbing pain?

No one noticed how I sank back
away from their lesson, nose close
to the all-purpose carpet. As Mr. Carbone
washed his hands, only I knew the battle
in my head, a vermillion fading.
We lined up for the march back to our room.

Blackberries at 40

I collect them in a cereal bowl
behind my mother's house, the way
I can't collect her thoughts. Easy berries
between my thumb and index finger,
they plump into my palm,
some so sweet they've lost their sassy sheen.

Brambles sprawl along her driveway,
margin scribbles to meet concrete.
Most things rural have gone,
but not these childhood mouthfuls,
their shadow-caves my oldest hiding place.
Eating as many as I pick, I ignore

the plenty of spindly pricks.
I love them. I don't want to go inside
to a parent's creeping decline.
Berry after berry, one should expect
thorns in a lifetime-forgetting,
the middle of the thicket dense

as when a prince crashes through 100 years.
Caught in this purple circus of berries,
I lack valor; I have only destiny: my tongue
squashes misplaced sorrow. No one left to warn me.
The dark fairy was always Amnesia.
Sugar and loss, I swallow and swallow.

Wilma's Bracelet

My aunt's charm bracelet jingles
when I lift it from my jewelry box:
dime-sized Edwards and Victorias,
pre-1900. Twenty-two lost likenesses,
features worn from faces, dates barely visible,
Dei Gratia Regina or *Rex Imperator,*
small O's welded above each head,

coins turned charms. My aunt pressed it
into my palm, weeks before she died.
For days, my fingers smelled like money,
a pickle jar of change, novelty,
the life she gathered wandering, bohemian,
while our family, scowling, shook their heads
and cared for her baby.

Where did she buy it? This bracelet
of likenesses, little kings and queens
with their haloes of attachment
heavy on my wrist. A big-picture person,
she never noticed details, or spoke of them.
Sometimes I see her reflection in mine,
finding old money in coat pockets.

Fourth Row Down, Sixth Face from the Left

Naval Training Class, San Diego, 1946

Post-Enola Gay, these Cold War fathers
line up in sailor suits. Fresh-shaven heads
sporting silly caps, white and crisp like paper boats.
154 cadets seem almost alike. I find my dad.
He faced the camera, afloat with these young men,
fourth row down, sixth face from the left.

But the problem remains, I've enlisted late,
too late to talk to him, over the sharp commands
that death brings. Why he never spoke of war
is a speck on the lens, or a whisper camped
in the Smirnoff's corrugated cardboard box
I'm unpacking now. We label what we can.

V

Diagnosis of Anorexia During the Annual Reading of Great Expectations

Somewhere in the middle of Dickens
she begins to thin. One cannot *grow* thin
any more than a blacksmith's boy
can become a gentleman.
She loses into her condition:

a wad of bread for lunch, marsh mist for supper,
forty pages in lieu of dessert. As the convict adopts Pip,
the empty ache consumes her. She takes it in,
loves it, breathes it. A seashell's empty calories
rush her ears, that whooshing fix of hunger.

With their pallid cheeks and protruding eyes,
characters show no sympathy—the newborn gentleman's
finery to die for—happiness should belong to him
who loses everything for a chance at greatness.
And the girl, Reader, the girl cannot be seen,

as mercenary cousins plot and jockey for jewels,
she spies through text's keyhole
tape measure looped around her thigh.
A cascade of Belgium lace here, a bottle of port there—
in this book luxury clings to cruelty.

Nothing tastes good anymore. Look how
pride turns a woman to ash.

Singing Dickinson

When I learned almost every one
of Emily Dickinson's poems
can be sung to "The Yellow Rose of Texas,"
I became uncomfortable with music. It surges up
when I want to make a point, or lurks in the background
invading my space. At measured intervals,
it jogs my brain to thoughts I do not want to think again.

"Mood Indigo" or "Orange Colored Sky" blared from our radio.
My father could not drive without his jazz.
I sat behind his alcoholic haze and cursed familiar tunes
that reminded me of other drives and silence
and things I could not say. Mom called his music noise,
but when she played piano and sang Cole Porter,
her melancholy crooned throughout my day.

I regret my parents' musical ways,
those notes tossed back so thoughtlessly.
That a poem could sacrifice itself to song
disheartens me, especially now, with a ten-year-old
singing Dickinson in our living room, her bell tones
more joyful than the words, causing the poem to shrink
soberly on its page, meter ticking.

On Conservatory Water

for Marcia Lipson

The sailboats on Conservatory Water
move for wind and hands, sure and remote.
My son guides one, his antenna wand
a ray of silver aimed toward a brownstone ledge
where hawks nest. He toggles left and right;
his vessel tacks across the pond
following sky's soft breath.

Near here, five years ago my friend died,
heart weakened from diabetes.
On a noontime walk, she paused to help
a stranger see two peregrine falcons.
She raised her arm to where the roosting pair
held court—trajectory true as a chapel ceiling,
and stopped breathing.

I like to think a raptor's eye took her in,
that moment—vision crossed in perfect
geometry, her index finger sure as a slice
of wing. Its unplanned dive another path
now, a ripple, as my son concentrates:
sailboats' masts point into firmament,
then cloth billows its life-sprint.

In the Cheetah Enclosure

Born captive, the cheetahs in the National Zoo do not understand
escape. There's little to tempt them. Even the zebra in the adjacent
pen remains a distant, moving wallpaper, checkered in chain-
link, an optical puzzle far from Namibia. Lulled by domestic,
North American asylum, the fast cats wait—unlike urban deer in
Washington, who are branching out. Dull-toothed and doe-eyed,
deer think they own the place, their border bleeding across busy
parkways, through senators' yards. A zoo volunteer explains that
sometimes at night deer jump into the cheetah enclosure, where
they find their end—run down by the fastest animal on Earth,
torn limb-from-limb. Zookeepers say the chase is good for the
cheetah, but not the flesh and blood and bone. Cheetahs gorge,
then vomit all back up again, unable to digest raw venison. An
intern removes the mess and tests the meat for parasites. Was it
close to where these school children stand, a deer's last ignorance?
Science. Nature. Tragic curiosity. The deer too slow to know
surprise or pain, the odds of a predator in their neck of the woods,
insane. A bounding arc of meat, its body falls. The cheetah darts
instinctively, outside geography. Something in Africa shrieks, as
thoughts land here.

Mute Swans

Our guide tells us to touch the eggs,
implying the mother swan won't mind.
And she flies off, churning a fuss
of water over the cattails.

Soft gray shells exposed, cygnets floating trapped,
I stroke the silenced weight,
brittle case, warm as something dangerous.
Knowing the parent swans could break my arm,

I wait for birth as though it were my own,
linger by the nest, until I see our guide off-shore. He flaps
his arms and points to wingtips hushing clouds
back from the east. His motion

and the motion of the swans strike silence deep
until it aches like fear, this feeling
like a weapon honed to stab, sharp as bone,
or voice held back and whitening with rage.

Pile of Discarded Shoes

Holocaust Museum, Washington, DC

Unnaturally older than their owners,
nothing like the leather they were,

strangely limp and wrinkled,
they hold each other—toe-to-toe

or heel-to-instep—not a metaphor
but evidence. Their emptiness aches

as if to separate feet from shoes itself
were brutal. Phantom metatarsals

sharpen themselves on disbelief.
An era away from Nazi death ovens,

their brown tongues and black knotty laces
burn my vision until I tear and wonder

if I am too young to be authentically
bitter or grieved. Behind glass

in semi-darkness, they prove a mountain
of distressed humanity, footprints lost

yet preserved, in each sole,
an archive of flesh memory.

Bad Dog, Memory

All the time you're telling it to stay,
it drools for a reward,
eager to scramble off with its bone
to a private corner of your mind.

Mornings, you wake to its howling
at garbage men who've come to take
rubbish from the curb of your dreams.
You curse its protective racket.

Later, when it's curled up tightly,
whuffling, foot-kicking, soft-jowled;
or at your heels, secret rock-eater,
tongue dripping—you love it.

Forgive lost collars, prized dead crabs,
its late return, limp cat
in its jaws. It whines
at your displeasure but barks at joy.

Cacophonous past,
beyond obedience,
old and full of tricks:
Take it by the choke chain.

Bluegill

Zipping down a wake of blond tendrils,
his bronze catch is sun-glanced—bluegill.
My boy's rod bent as a bow, to spring
as his wrist jolts life to air.
The fish flies onto grass, gasps.

I'm the only grown-up to see
its thrashing portrait in lavender;
its platinum frame the size of my hand.
I imagine the hook in its lip and cringe.
Clearly, we'll throw it back.

Kneeling on the bank with my son,
we hold the line tight, and I reach
my finger into the fish mouth, but no fisherman,
I jerk away at its pinch. My son says,
Put your foot on it, but I can't.

It's trapped, panicked, flailing,
close to death. I can almost imagine its pain.
The mouth's swallowed lure
chains me to the reel, a breathless place,
a boot pressed on my spine.

Another adult comes to save the day—
a handy tackle box, he cuts the line,
and the fish, like a manic bar of soap,
flops free to muddy shallows,
keeping its hook, an alloy scar,

with a thread of captivity trailing
down its jaw, a badge of misfortune
just barely escaped. Its bluegill-life
resumes almost accidentally.

Why I Cry When I Read My Children
Lassie, Come Home

Because that ginger and white collie flashed across rural America,
    a sheriff's flare for right and wrong.
Because before her broadcast fame, she struggled back to people
    who had nothing.
Because Lassie knows where she is supposed to be.

Because dog hairs still cling to splintered floors.
Because of elusive liberty.
Because far north on the map, the collie's a long-suffering speck, paws
    torn, senses tortured in a country grown rugged with miles.

Because four-o-clock torments her.
Because she never pees on the page.
Because when death is near, Lassie delivers herself.

Because of the father's coal-mine cough.
Because of the mother's soft blue apron.
Because the child Joe is Lassie's.

Because the Lord can't buy man's best friend.
Because flannel pajamas absorb a good cry.
Because fighting nostalgia we make our way in the world.

ABOUT THE AUTHOR

KATHI MORRISON-TAYLOR was born and raised in the Pacific Northwest. She completed her MFA at the University of Washington in 1989 and since then has lived in California, Connecticut, and Virginia. Her poems have appeared in *Southern Poetry Review, Stand, Connecticut River Review, Seattle Review,* and *New York Quarterly,* among other magazines. Co-director of the Joaquin Miller Cabin Reading Series in Washington, DC, she has worked both as a teacher and librarian. She and her husband and two children make their home in Arlington, Virginia.

ABOUT THE ARTIST

GRIER TORRENCE holds an MFA from Yale School of Art and a BFA from Rhode Island School of Design. He began exhibiting his work in the 1970s, including Babcock Galleries (NYC), Alpha Gallery (Boston) and Gallery 100 (Saratoga Springs). Teaching posts have included Pratt Institute and Southern Connecticut State College. He lives with wife and two daughters in Farmington, CT and teaches at Miss Porter's School. Visit his website at www.griertorrence.com.

ABOUT THE HTC COLLECTION

The HILARY THAM CAPITAL COLLECTION (HTC COLLECTION) is an imprint by THE WORD WORKS that features excellence in poetry from authors in the Greater Washington, DC area. The hallmark of this series is that each book selected is financially supported by advance book sales and community contributions. The author also agrees to work with the press to promote the HTC Collection books, support other activities of The Word Works, and increase public interest in poetry.

In 1989, Hilary Tham was the first author published in the Capital Collection imprint. In 1994, when she became Word Works Editor-in-Chief, she revitalized the imprint, which had produced only two titles. By June 2005, Ms. Tham had paved the way for publication of thirteen additional Capital Collection titles.

The following individuals and organizations have contributed to the HTC Collection to make this book possible:

PATRONS: J. H. Beall • Miles David Moore • Marchant Wentworth

DONORS: Dominica Borg • W. Perry Epes • Robert L. Giron • Paul Grayson • Rosalia Rodriguez-Garcia • Bill Taylor & Nancy Uding

FRIENDS: Sarah Browning • Christopher Conlon • Alice DeLana • Ellen Harder • Myong-Hee Kim • Susan Mockler • Rhoda Trooboff • Jane Whitaker • Betsy Wollaston

Thanks to our generous anonymous contributors.

ABOUT THE WORD WORKS

The WORD WORKS, a nonprofit literary organization, publishes contemporary poetry in collectors' editions. Since 1981, the organization has sponsored the Washington Prize, a $1,500 award to an American poet. Monthly, The Word Works presents free literary programs in the Chevy Chase Café Muse series, and each summer, free poetry programs are held at the historic Joaquin Miller Cabin in Washington, DC's Rock Creek Park. Annually, two high school students debut in the Miller Cabin Series as winners of the Jacklyn Potter Young Poets Competition.

Since 1974, WORD WORKS programs have included "In the Shadow of the Capitol," a symposium and archival project on the African-American intellectual community in segregated Washington, DC; the Gunston Arts Center Poetry Series (Ai, Carolyn Forché, Stanley Kunitz, and others); the Poet-Editor panel discussions at the Bethesda Writer's Center (John Hollander, Maurice English, Anthony Hecht, Josephine Jacobsen, and others); Poet's Jam, a multi-arts program series featuring poetry in performance; a poetry workshop at the Center for Creative Non-Violence (CCNV) shelter; and the Arts Retreat in Tuscany. Master Class workshops, an ongoing program, have featured Agha Shahid Ali, Thomas Lux, and Marilyn Nelson.

In 2009, WORD WORKS will have published 67 titles, including work from such authors as Deirdra Baldwin, J.H. Beall, Christopher Bursk, John Pauker, Edward Weismiller, and Mac Wellman. Currently, The Word Works publishes books and occasional anthologies under three imprints: the Washington Prize, the Hilary Tham Capital Collection, and International Editions.

Past grants have been awarded by the National Endowment for the Arts, National Endowment for the Humanities, DC Commission on the Arts & Humanities, Witter Bynner Foundation, Writer's Center, Bell Atlantic, Batir Foundation, and others, including many generous private patrons.

The WORD WORKS has established an archive of artistic and administrative materials in the Washington Writing Archive housed in the George Washington University Gelman Library.

Please enclose a self-addressed, stamped envelope with all inquiries.

The Word Works   PO Box 42164   Washington, DC 20015
editor@wordworksdc.com   www.wordworksdc.com

WORD WORKS BOOKS

Karren L. Alenier, Hilary Tham, Miles David Moore, EDS.,
Winners: A Retrospective of the Washington Prize

* Nathalie F. Anderson, *Following Fred Astaire*

* Michael Atkinson, *One Hundred Children Waiting for a Train*

Mel Belin, *Flesh That Was Chrysalis* (HTC COLLECTION)

* Carrie Bennett, *biography of water*

* Peter Blair, *Last Heat*

Doris Brody, *Judging the Distance* (HTC COLLECTION)

Sarah Browning, *Whiskey in the Garden of Eden* (HTC COLLECTION)

* Richard Carr, *Ace*

Christopher Conlon, *Gilbert and Garbo in Love* (HTC COLLECTION)

Christopher Conlon, *Mary Falls* (HTC COLLECTION)

Donna Denizé, *Broken Like Job* (HTC COLLECTION)

Moshe Dor, Barbara Goldberg, Giora Leshem, EDS.,
The Stones Remember

James C. Hopkins, *Eight Pale Women* (HTC COLLECTION)

James C. Hopkins & Yoko Danno, *The Blue Door*
(INTERNATIONAL EDITIONS)

Brandon D. Johnson, *Love's Skin* (HTC COLLECTION)

Myong-Hee Kim, *Crow's Eye View: The Infamy of Lee Sang,
Korean Poet* (INTERNATIONAL EDITIONS)

Vladimir Levchev, *Black Book of the Endangered Species*
(INTERNATIONAL EDITIONS)

* Richard Lyons, *Fleur Carnivore*

* Fred Marchant, *Tipping Point*

Judith McCombs, *The Habit of Fire* (HTC COLLECTION)

* Ron Mohring, *Survivable World*

Miles David Moore, *The Bears of Paris* (HTC COLLECTION)

Miles David Moore, *Rollercoaster* (HTC COLLECTION)

Jacklyn Potter, Dwaine Rieves, Gary Stein, EDS.
Cabin Fever: Poets at Joaquin Miller's Cabin

* Jay Rogoff, *The Cutoff*

Robert Sargent, *Aspects of a Southern Story*

Robert Sargent, *A Woman From Memphis*

* Prartho Sereno, *Call from Paris*

* Enid Shomer, *Stalking the Florida Panther*

* John Surowiecki, *The Hat City After Men Stopped Wearing Hats*

Maria Terrone, *The Bodies We Were Loaned* (HTC COLLECTION)

Hilary Tham, *Bad Names for Women* (HTC COLLECTION)

Hilary Tham, *Counting* (HTC COLLECTION)

Jonathan Vaile, *Blue Cowboy* (HTC COLLECTION)

* Miles Waggener, *Phoenix Suites*

Rosemary Winslow, *Green Bodies* (HTC COLLECTION)

* WASHINGTON PRIZE WINNERS